CW00858374

Values Count:

Believing in what we do

Stuart Eglin, PhD

Stuart Eglin

Values Count

Stuart Eglin

Values Count:

Believing in What We Do

A book about values based working by Stuart Eglin

blue*water* books

Stuart Eglin

blue*water books*

Website at: www.stuarteglin.com

Email at: stuart@stuarteglin.com

Blog at: www.stuarteglin.com/blog

This edition published in 2017.

Copyright © Stuart Eglin 2017

bw101

Values Count

Stuart Eglin

TABLE OF CONTENTS

Stuart Eglin

Introduction

It's all about the money — that seems to be the measure by which everything is judged these days. Every day we hear about new scandals relating to the ethical basis of business, whether it's large multi-national companies not paying their taxes or corporates who distort their accounts to massage the stock market, or banks that lend irresponsibly and then look to governments to bail them out when they are at risk of collapsing. Too big to fail was a mantra that was all over the newspapers a few years ago. Those of us who work in the public sector are not exempt from these problems.

In recent years there has been a growing rhetoric that says "private sector good, public sector bad". This manifests itself in neo-liberal politics where the market rules and public sector provision is seen as intrinsically inefficient. We increasingly live in a world that knows the price of everything without any underlying sense of the value of what we do.

Looking at the backdrop of this, we live in a world of contradictions — both spectacularly devoid of values, whilst also bringing forward new concepts that do have deeper value sets. Some of the recent global phenomena we have seen, such as online petition sites, micro-lending initiatives and crowd sourcing, for example — do look like they are setting out from a place of deep value and an intention to improve the world in which they are operating. In a career that spans some 25 years working in the British health service, and before that 7 years in a charity — I have worked in many different organisations. As a coach I have also worked alongside people from the university sector and from small businesses. Looking at what drives people in the workplace is fascinating. At some point in any coaching conversation that develops with a client there will emerge a sense that the "career" needs to fulfil something deeper for the client. Sometimes the client will feel that they have given up on any deeper sense that they are striving for something, they will feel that it is impossible to satisfy that need.

When this point emerges, I will often use a model that I came across many years ago on a blog by Dave Pollard (called 'How to Save the World). The model looks like this:

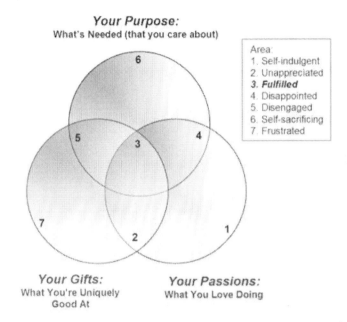

Source: Dave Pollard – Finding the Sweet Spot

Pollard describes the point in the middle as the "Sweet Spot" that we are all wanting to identify. This model doesn't intrinsically look at the issue of values. But it is a really good way to begin the conversation that opens up when we look at what we really want to be doing, what we are good at, and what other people want from us.

Put simply, if we pursue that sweet spot at the middle of the circle without thinking about our impact on the world around us, we act without any ethical basis. That will leave us empty inside, yearning for something more. This is why values are so important.

Over recent years, I have become more conscious of the underlying drivers to the way that I work. For example, when making complex decisions where there is no right answer - what are the factors that determine which decision I will take? How do I decide which work to do and which to let go of? One thing has become really clear - the key driver is not money. Even when I had a young family to support, it was difficult to make decisions about jobs and career based just on who paid the most.

The target of fulfilment, or as Jung might label it, self-actualisation - is driven by something deeper. Jung argued that it is part of our psychological hardwiring that we spend our entire lives going from a splitting of characteristics and onward to pulling everything back together again through a process of individuation. Literally, we are putting ourselves back together again, realizing who we are and understanding what our contribution is to the world. Whether we are the leader of a huge corporation or the person who cleans the front doorway, how we embrace each day and how we show up to everyone we encounter shows clearly where we are on this journey of understanding.

Over the last decade I have often found myself articulating the ways in which I wanted things to be done. This often felt like I was describing an inner wisdom, something where I would intrinsically want to describe how things should be, even when I wasn't sure where or why this came about. It would take the form of statements about why we were doing a particular piece of work, who we should include in it, how we should negotiate, how we should show up in the workspace.

I was intrigued as to where this was coming from, and what its purpose was. For the last ten years I have been leading a team of people who have been developing research capability and capacity in healthcare in the North West of England. I was keen to identify the impact our work was having. I commissioned an Impact Project in 2011, which was carried out by two people, Nick and Sue, who developed an approach which was based on a series of stakeholder interviews, underpinned by data and outputs. It was the founding work that has led to the thinking in Beyond Measurement, a programme of work I have been gestating for a while now. This work still has a way to go yet – looking at how to identify underlying values that support a work programme and go beyond more bottom line concepts like value for money and return on investment.

One of the really interesting things to emerge from the work came from a series of interviews that Nick and Sue did with core members of the team. I spent three afternoons exploring with them what the key features were which were leading to successful programmes of work, and what some of the factors were that were creating work that was not productive.

Through these discussions we developed a framework together. This was tested out in further conversations. Within the framework were key values. Sue and Nick identified 6 of them. They were:

Altruism

Integrity

Co-creation

Inclusivity

Humility

Optimism

We explored these in some depth. Since that work was carried out, these values have really helped me to articulate the drivers in the work that I do. They were revisited again in the second impact report in 2013, where there was an opportunity to sense-check them through the massive organisational change we had experienced in the NHS in England.

Then, last year, as I put together a new team to take the work forward - we had a further session looking at what these values meant for us all. It was a session which really helped to bring us together as a team. In the last few months we embarked on a team process developed by Professor Michael West. Called, the Aston OD Team Journey, it takes the team through a structured programme of work that is aimed at developing a highly effective team. At the time of writing, we are part way through the journey and have just completed a process looking at the team behaviours that we value. With this, we took the six core values that we had identified and worked together to identify the kind of behaviours we wanted to see that would underpin these values. We identified these behaviours as:

1.   We have written down goals, co-created and agreed on an annual basis and reviewed regularly by the whole team.

2.   We work together within the team and stakeholders to openly encourage new ideas with optimism and a "can do" attitude. We set aside time and space to discuss and explore new ideas, identify and acknowledge those that can be incorporated into our work.

3.   We create a friendly atmosphere by talking to each other, laughing together, smiling, showing an interest in each other, welcoming new people and having a kind and caring attitude.

4.   We listen to each other and provide advice and support.

5. We value, attend and contribute to regular team meetings. We endeavour to keep each other informed between meetings about our work.

6. We are open, honest and respectful in all that we do by listening to what others have to say, appreciating and considering others' points of view, respecting difference. We recognise that conflict and resolution is part of a healthy team.

7. We provide the opportunity via team meetings, appraisals, one-to-one and informal discussions for everyone to identify and articulate what they want and need to do their job.

8. We provide the opportunity for all team members to develop personally and professionally through formal/informal training, mentoring, etc.

9. We will improve the way we recognise, celebrate and reward achievements.

10. We agree, record and complete actions and review progress taking into account the broader priorities and competing demands affecting delivery.

11.   We organise our work so that it is of high quality and delivered within agreed time frames.

The rest of this book will look more broadly at values within the workplace. Taking the work I have developed with my own team as the starting point, we will look at other examples of value-based approaches. We will also look at practical approaches to developing a value set individually and in teams. In the later chapters of the book I will go on to look at some of the more theoretical approaches that have helped to shape my own approach to values-based working.

Stuart Eglin
Liverpool
September, 2016

Chapter 1
Developing Core Values – an example

Value 1 – Altruism

Earlier in this book I talked about the work I have been leading over the last few years and the way in which this has been underpinned by a set of core values. I also referred to two reports that we commissioned which looked at the impact of our work. As part of that study, these core values were explicitly set out. They were derived from a set of conversations with the researchers. Here then, is the first of those values, Altruism. In the first report it was set out like this:

2011: Altruism. In this context, it describes an approach which focuses on delivering results without seeking personal credit or glory. There is a strong focus on results and supporting and developing others to achieve success.

This was a strong driver in our work. A constant reminder that work becomes undermined by the presence of ego. When we get out of our own way, we can achieve remarkable things. But to do this, we need to be able to totally focus on the desired outcome and leave to one side any sense of the need for glory.

Last year's report provided an opportunity to look again at each value and see what progress had been made.

2013: Altruism. This is reflected in the 'gentle, non threatening, public service focus that stakeholders have described. For this team it is about "delivering results without seeking personal credit or glory." The quote was taken from an interview with one of our key stakeholders. This value is still fundamental to what I believe. But the last 2 years has seen a significant shift in the culture of the NHS as a result of changes in the structures and incentives. It is now very difficult to have this outcome focus without an acknowledgement of the need for recognition of the value of the work. Putting it bluntly, if the funder doesn't know we did it why would they pay us to do more?

So, what does this do to the underlying value? Well, within the new regime in which we work I do think that the principle I set out above about needing to keep ego out of the work that we do is still a fundamental that underlines all that we do. The challenge is in looking at how we add value to the system and ensuring that there is an acknowledgement of the value of the work without us needing to step forward for praise. This dilemma reminds me of the words of Lao Tzu:

A leader is best
When people barely know he exists

Of a good leader, who talks little,
When his work is done, his aim fulfilled,
They will say, "We did this ourselves."

The NHS as it is set out since the Health Reforms of the Coalition government here in the UK, does not lend itself to the approach advocated by Lao Tzu in the Tao Teh Ching. Instead, the principles of competition are being seen as a force for change. Unfortunately that creates sets of very unhelpful incentives that don't facilitate the co-operation, collaboration and integration that is needed in healthcare to ensure that the quality of care delivered is as excellent as it can be.

Where does this leave our aspirations for this first value? If anything, it is even more important to adhere to this value. Values run deep - and I for one have a strong allegiance to the reference to "public service" in the quote referred to earlier. However, whilst the value needs to be applied to ensure that we are focused on what we achieve rather than on receiving credit for what we do - there is still a need to avoid being naive and ensure that we demonstrate the value of our work through the assessment work we have commissioned like the reports of 2011 and 2013.

It is also worth looking at how we measure in more detail. I have been looking at more complex and subtle measures of our impact. Through subtle measures we will be able to determine the impact of our work from a non-ego perspective.

Culture is notoriously difficult to change - the focus of our work has been on generating cultures that are responsive to research and innovation. The tricky bit in all of this is figuring out how to measure culture change, how to come up with measures that give value without reducing everything to something that can be counted. Sure, it is important to take account of Return on Investment and there is a place for Cost Benefit Analysis. And we have done Health Economics analysis of our impact too.

But what about more subtle measures?

I have had some fascinating conversations with people - disciplines have included sociology, linguistics, psychology and anthropology. I have been searching for ways of determining shifts in culture brought about by work that we have been doing with people. There was a really interesting conference in 2013 run by the Social Impact Analysts Association in Paris that looked beyond measurement. The paper from the conference is full of fascinating ideas.

This work on measurement is a work in progress. I am looking for ways to demonstrate the intrinsic value of things that are not reduced to crude measures. To coin a phrase, I want to get to the deep values of the things that we do, rather than just the cash value of it.

In conversation with someone involved in the arts recently, I pointed out that over the centuries when great works of art, great music and great works of architecture were being developed - we did not keep asking what the return on investment was. We were content to see the value of something as defined by its own instrinsic aesthetic. So, learning from this - I am looking for a way to develop our set of values and indicators that are derived from what we are setting out to do, rather than from some arbitrary external measure. It's proving to be an absorbing and fascinating journey.

Value 2 - integrity

In looking at Integrity it probably helps to look at the descriptions that were set out in the two Impact Reports that illustrated the application of these values. In the first report, in 2011 integrity was described as: stakeholders acknowledge the fairness and openness in the way that the team works with people. In 2013 it was described thus: stakeholders have identified the independent and impartial approach the team has. This reflects their open style and the 'broker role' they are seen to play.

In developing this honest broker role, it has been vital to demonstrate absolute integrity in the way in which we work. This value works well with altruism as the key facet in a framework of values. So, how does this work, and would you really have an organisation that positively supported lack of integrity? Well, the idea of an overt lack of integrity is difficult to imagine, but there are certainly organisations where the main aim is to win at all cost. And there are plenty of organisations where the primary focus is the profit motive, and any broader concerns would be secondary to that.

In giving attention to Integrity we are looking for ways of operating that maintain an honest approach that is aimed at leaving the world better than we found it. There also needs to be a focus on being transparent to all, not playing people off against each other. This doesn't imply that by behaving in this way we are open to being manipulated. Any work within and between organisations has a political dimension to it. When I hear people say that they can't stand office politics and try to stay away from it, I think they are describing a desire to avoid negative politics such as gossip, bullying and victimising. But it is not possible to be completely removed from politics. In any organisation there is a need for people to interact and for them to build levels of trust. This requires interactions that lead to an outcome. By focusing on Integrity, those interactions should function with a positive intent. We are not all out for what we can get out of things. Taking Integrity as a fundamental value enables us to work to a common goal and not for our own ends. Working in the public sector and in health care, our focus should be kindness and mindfulness. We ensure that those we encounter are improved through the interaction. These sound like bold requirements - but if they are addressed with humility, it is possible to build a reputation as a team that delivers, and a team that has Integrity, that can be trusted.

Ultimately, if we are seen as a team that can be relied on to work for a greater good than its own ends, we will be able to work in ambitious ways beyond our immediate parameters. The ambition then can be to go for the audacious goals, and take people with us.

Value 3 – Co-creation

Let us now look at the role of Co-creation in our work. In the two Impact Reports the team's approach is described as being underpinned by collaborative working, which works on co-creation. This is a very fashionable term. Many organisations, particularly in the public sector talk about co-creation or co-production. In many cases the term is used very loosely. However, in many cases, organisations actually mean that they bring a pre-developed idea for some shared work on its delivery. This is not true co-creation.

When I use the term, I am talking about an approach to creating new projects that begins with a very broad idea and very quickly gets into a co-creation space. When we commission people to work with us, we expect them to bring their expertise to the design stage. This may mean that the brief changes completely from the start-up phase through to execution. The traditional way to commission work is to define the specification and be really clear about all aspects of it before engaging the people who are going to deliver the work. This is fine when you have all of the answers, but limited if you are intending to engage experts who have ideas that wouldn't occur to you before you connect with them. For this reason, we look where possible to make sure that we do not restrict the journey that the project will travel as it is developed.

Intrinsic in this approach is an understanding that we not only trust the people who we work with, but also that we respect the expertise and knowledge that they bring to the process and fully expect them to know things that we don't and to have a perspective that is fresh.

This core value is key to ensuring an innovative approach to work, where there is always space for reflection and to draw on the ideas of the whole team of people who are involved. To do this, we need to be prepared to look at anything - whilst maintaining focus through being clear about the core vision of what we are setting out to achieve.

Adhering to these principles creates an environment where it is possible to truly co-create. It also ensures that the work programme that we deliver is not reliant on a small team, but can draw on a much wider group of people who sign up to the core

Stuart Eglin

values of the ways in which we work. We have achieved this by creating a group of Associates that we call Faculty, who are not employed as part of the team, but do help with creating our work and contribute to the wider development of our overall programmes.

Value 4 - Inclusivity

So far, we have looked at the values of Altruism, Integrity and Co-Creation. This section looks at Inclusivity. This relates to the recognition that ensuring people are involved and included is a key aspect of our work. This core value complements the previous value of co-creation. To enable co-creation it is important to be inclusive.

Working in the world of health research, this value is not without controversy. It sits at the heart of the conflict between approaches to research that strive at excellence and those that set out to see a thousand flowers bloom. Whilst I appreciate the importance of excellence in achieving high quality, it is vital to ensure that work is inclusive. Instinctively it feels right to include people wherever possible in things that we do. The default when asking whether someone should be in the room, is to say yes. There have to be really good reasons to leave someone out!

As I have said, this can make us at odds with those that set out to achieve centres of high excellence and work with exclusivity.

Still, if we are to build excellence into all that we do, we need to draw on the expertise of others. If we exclude people, we limit the ability to draw on wide areas of expertise.

This is why this core value drives what we do. Again, if we look at the way in which the values complement each other, if we work from an understanding that all of the expertise is not held within the team, and that we need to draw on skills from others - by being inclusive, we increase the chances that we will succeed. Thus, as we look across the health professionals and look at the ways in which research is conducted in healthcare - there is far too much emphasis on trials led by medics. This is the outcome of exclusivity. As a result we miss out on the wider perspectives that research needs which can be brought to the agenda by the other professions that work in healthcare. By being inclusive and working particularly to include those professions that are very under-represented in research, we can create an environment where the richness of research is much much deeper.

Value 5 - Humility

When the team I work with evaluated back in 2011, the value of humility was described as a non-hierarchical, respectful, modest style; a style which supports others to contribute.

This is a key part of the style and culture that underpins our work. We work with partners to deliver projects where the key factor is the success of the project, rather than our profile. We have always been more concerned about the contents of the shop, rather than having a glossy shop window. At times, this has given us problems - but the underlying focus on humility is a key strength of our work. I have talked in earlier posts in this series about the importance of the "honest broker" role that we play. It is very difficult to act in this role if partners have any sense that the work is being done for greater glory or self-aggrandisement. In the last couple of years, the NHS has had a much greater emphasis on the market and on competition rather than collaboration. This has, at times, made it very difficult to work from a place of humility whilst all around are vying for position.

Ultimately though the best dressed window, the most impressive marketing campaign, is nothing if the contents of delivery are not of the highest quality.

As with so many things, the middle way will help tackle this tension. So, it is important not to be naive about the need to ensure that others understand the role and scope of the team in delivery of its work. This can be done without overplaying the 'publicity campaign'. Ultimately, it's a question of getting the work recognised to ensure that it continues without the ego getting in the way.

Working from a place of humility ensures that the objective is to serve others and deliver something of the highest quality that is of great value to those with whom we work.

Value 6 – Optimism

The thing about a cliché is that it becomes a cliché because it has currency. So, that well-trodden expression: "are you a glass half empty or a glass half full person" does have substance to it. The world seems to be divided into these two categories - those that see what is missing in life, and those that celebrate what they actually have. Taken an optimistic outlook on life is a key element of the values I am setting out, because it creates the tone for the other values. Looking optimistically at any situation creates a real can-do attitude, an approach that believes there is a positive solution to any situation. It is also the basis from which to work with an "owner" state of mind. Chris Brogan talks extensively about the owner. It's the opposite of being a victim. When we own our reality, and are prepared to tackle any situation and look for a solution, we are creating the causes for success. Even when things are not going well, it is possible to see an optimistic position - things could be worse, at least we don't have to sort that out, at least we can make some choices, there's a lot to learn from this situation. There are always positive ways to look at any situation. It is also interesting to see how adopting an optimistic value set can be infectious. For a start, when we are optimistic about the possible outcome in a situation, others will adopt that attitude with us - willing us to succeed. Sometimes it is possible to create a more optimistic reality in the future by talking it up and getting others to believe that it will happen. Overcoming barriers and obstacles by having a strong conviction of optimism can actually help the barriers to disappear. A dogged belief in the future is what gets so many successful people to achieve the seemingly impossible.

What do I mean when I talk about this dogged belief? It's to do with being unreasonable for a legitimate reason.

This quote helps (it's from George Bernard Shaw):

"The reasonable man adapts himself to the world. The unreasonable one persists in trying to adapt the world to himself. Therefore, all progress depends on the unreasonable man."

OK, allowing for the sexist language (Shaw was writing some time ago!) — it's a brilliant quote. It helps me to stay connected to the ideas that I have been working on for the last few years. Protecting my ideas from toxic influences is really key to this.

When I am accused of being unreasonable in my expectations, when someone says to me that my ambitions are unrealistic in the current economic climate, I say that it is through being unreasonable (in a way that is congruous with my values) that I will make real progress.

Even whilst all around is crumbling and falling apart, there is a key place for unfaltering optimism. If we look deep within, that optimism is always there.

Stuart Eglin

Chapter 2
Ideas for Identifying our Values

We are now going to look in more detail at various approaches to identifying the core values that underpin what we do. This does not entail random generation of a set of terms that we think will fit the market, or that we think our customers or clients would want us to be describing. That would lack authenticity. Instead, this chapter will provide a set of techniques to help you to look in more depth at the values that already drive you and the people that you work with.

What drives you

When I first started to look at how I worked and what the key factors were that inspired me in the work that I did, there were some key things that started me on the journey.

It is unusual to have worked in a number of different places without having worked in a place that didn't feel right. We have all been there – that niggling feeling that the things that drive the place that we are working in just don't make us feel comfortable. Sometimes it's an ethical thing – a strong sense that the way the organisation does business is not right because it exploits or it has no scruples in the quest to make profit.

But sometimes it is not that clear-cut. There is still a lingering sense that we are not somewhere that we feel comfortable. Earlier in my career, as a part of a management development initiative I went through an assessment centre which included a set of personality profiles. Amongst these was the Career Anchors test. Developed by Edgar Schein in 1990, this simple test determines what the key dominant anchors are that will define the work context in which we are likely to be most happy, and to really thrive. There are eight sets of anchors :

Technical / Functional competence

General Managerial competence

Autonomy / Independence

Security / Stability

Entrepreneurial Creativity

Service / Dedication to a cause

Pure Challenge

Lifestyle

Being clear about the specific anchors that drive us is really important if we are to make wise choices in our career. This helps us too if we want to get in touch with the deeper values that determine how we engage with work. In my own coaching practice for example, I tend to find that clients who work in the public sector are strongly driven by the need to contribute, to benefit others and to make a difference. These strong urges are at the heart of their value base.

For some years I had been pretty clear about what the things were that mattered to me. I found myself articulating them to the teams I worked with when I was describing what I wanted to be done and how I wanted it to be done.

Saying to the team that I wanted to develop a new project, that it should be collaborative, that we are not there to compete with key partners. These are signs of the underpinning values that I was working with. Also, saying to colleagues that even when we were getting knock-backs and not making progress "that sounds to me like a not yet, rather than a simple no" — shows the strong level of optimism that drives the way in which I work.

So, listening for clues in the way we talk, the stories that we tell, can be a strong indicator of the values that we are working to.

Other clues include the way in which we make decisions, the work opportunities that particularly appeal to us, and the way in which we approach others.

If we are lucky to have experienced a 360° Feedback exercise there will also be a lot of material in there from the views that others have of the way in which we work. Usually these exercises are built around a competency framework that the organization works with, but there is also space for free text from subordinates, peers, line manager and our wider network of contacts. In this free text we will find many clues to the values that drive the way we work.

As I explained in the worked example in the last chapter, I was lucky enough to have semi-structured conversations with two people who we had commissioned to do an impact survey of our work. Through these long, recorded conversations came the benefit of having an objective analysis of the values that drive my approach as a leader.

Even if this is not available, there are plenty of ways to look at this and find clues to the values that underpin our work.

What got you here

Looking around us for clues can be a helpful way to get in touch with our core values. In addition, it is really useful if we can do some simple biography work to connect with the aspects of our lives that have shaped us.

What do I mean by biography work? Am I suggesting that we all need to write our biography as a book to truly understand our core values?

No, we don't need to go to that depth to properly understand the values that are at our core.

A simple biography mapping exercise can help us to understand some of the factors that have helped to shape us.

I first came across the idea of biography mapping in the 1990s when I was lucky enough to meet Dame Rennie Fritchie (now Baroness Fritchie). I arranged to meet Rennie as part of my research work for my PhD thesis. She was very generous in spending time with me and sharing her ideas about organisational change in healthcare. She had also recently published her ideas about biography mapping and shared the ideas with me. The approach I set out here is adapted from her work. It is a really powerful technique.

Working with a simple prompt sheet, we go through the questions one at a time. Each questions invites us to trace a particular part of our life story. The power of the exercise comes from the way it works from our beginnings to the present day and onwards into the future. The whole exercise works as a metaphor for seeing our life as a story that we are creating episode by episode.

The phases we go through are as follows:

PART ONE - Plotting the Stars

What kind of human being do you want to be?

Describe the kinds of skills, abilities, qualities, disposition, character and understanding you want to have.

What do you want to do with your life?

Think in large as well as small ways of achievements, actions and important issues for you.

PART TWO - Mapping the Journey

Where are you?

Describe fully your current stage, both personal and career.

How did you get there?

Look back in your life and trace all the elements, happenings and people who have influenced your life path.

Where do you want to go?

Using the material from 1 and 2 begin to describe your real intentions.

How will you get there?

Refer to the information you have gained about your journey in life so far and consider new ways

What will you do when you arrive?

Begin to sketch in your intentions and actions.

Where to next?

Life is a continuous process, so begin to look beyond your immediate horizons.

How do you begin?

PART THREE - Starting Out

Plan of action

Write out a plan of action to describe how you will turn this exercise into specific actions that will move you forwards.

It's an exercise that I would encourage you to attempt. It is also worth revisiting at regular intervals, say once a year, to see what progress we have made and to what extent our journey is following the path that we set.

There are three approaches that we can take to looking back. The elements of the exercise that look back and ask us to trace our path can be written out as a simple narrative.

However, it might be also really useful to try a couple of alternative approaches.

Mapping - with a large sheet of paper, we could use crayons or coloured pens to trace out the path we have followed. We can either set out a map in the form of a place, or we can use abstract symbols to represent episodes.

Illustrating the key events in our life that have shaped us along the way will help us to understand what these events are and how they have impacted on our beliefs about ourselves and about the world around us.

Charting – draw a chart on a piece of paper with specific events set out on it as they occurred through time. Each event can be depicted on the chart to show the extent to which they were positive or negative events. We might also want to show each event with symbols that depict why they were important.

All of this work on our personal development will help us to get a better understanding of the underpinning events that have shaped us into the person that we are today. It is not a mere coincidence that we hold the values that we do. They are shaped by a really wide range of factors and influences. Using language and images to analyse this helps us to get a broader grasp of what is going on.

Inner Dialogue Work

Having done the exercises in the previous section, it is now time to do some more work on the findings that you have produced.

A couple of simple techniques can be applied which will give you an even deeper insight. These two approaches involve using interviewing techniques and letter writing.

Firstly, take some of the material that you have generated from the mapping exercises. For example, take a specific episode that has significantly shaped your life. Set out an outline of that episode so that you can look for questions that might help to further understand why it has shaped you. Then, take time to go through the questions and interview yourself, recording your answers as you work through them.

Useful questions could include:

- Why have you identified this episode as important?

- How did the situation make you feel?

- What lessons did you learn from this situation?

These episodes can also be analysed using a simple letter writing technique. This is an opportunity to tap into the insight that we think we might get from someone who has been a significant influence on us.

Think of someone who has had this kind of influence on you. They could be living or dead, someone you have met, or someone you have read books by, or know about from the media. Once you have decided who to work with on this exercise, you write a short letter which sets out the situation and asks that person some questions that you think will help to give you insight.

Then, take about 20 minutes to write a letter of response, written as though you were that person. Try to imagine the response they would give you, the advice they would offer.

Until you try this exercise, it will feel somewhat artificial. But if you give it a try you will be surprised by the power of it. Somehow it does actually help you to tap into startling advice and perspectives. It is as though you are able to draw on the advice from that person.

Building values for a team

So far we have been looking in detail at how to tap into the core values that drive us as individuals. This is an important first step in the journey. However, none of us work in isolation. We are all interconnected. We rely on others to do what we need to do. Whether in work, or in play — whether we look at our work team or our home connections – we need to work with others to get things done.

So, the next step in this process is to use techniques to unpack a set of core values that are relevant to the team as a whole.

The approach I am suggesting for this is adapted from techniques used by Professor Michael West in his development of the Aston OD Team Journey process. It builds on a workshop which my team did with Taravandana Lupson, which looked at our core values and developed from them a set of key behaviours. It was a really engaging and powerful workshop.

Ask each member of the team to take about 10 minutes to think about an experience in their working life when they have been in a really effective team and where their experience was really positive. Using post-it notes, ask each person to write down at least 5 ways that they would describe the way that this team worked. In other words, we are looking for the values that the team displayed.

Once each person has their list of 5 characteristics, invite them to work in pairs and compare the characteristics they have produced. Between them they will now develop a single list that removes any duplication or overlap. Then capture all of the characteristics from the team. Look to group them if that is possible. From this there should emerge some key values that represent the way that the team wants to work together. In chapter two I then went described how the team I work with took the 6 core values and translated them into key behaviours that reflect those values. This is a key step as it creates a set of sentences that describe behaviours that can be seen. Thus, it becomes possible to check whether the core values are being adhered to.

Who else are we like?

Typically, the group exercise described above is a powerful and straightforward way to identify a set of core values for the team.

Sometimes the team may have difficulties reaching agreement, or there may be significant problems in developing a coherent list. If this happens it might be worth giving the team time to reflect on the team's approach in a bit more detail. One way of doing this is to cast around and see if there are other teams or organisations that the team sees itself as similar to. If there are, it may be easier to reflect on how that other team works. Sometime it is easier to look outwards and do some reflection on another team rather than our own.

This approach can be used if the previous exercise becomes stuck for one reason or another. Then, looking outwards can give us new ideas to work with.

This technique can also be used to compare the results produced if the team manages the exercise in the previous section without a problem. Identifying another team that is like us gives us the opportunity to compare and contrast – and that may throw up some more ideas about the values that underpin our work.

Adopting or adapting another system

We live in a world where it is so easy to find solutions to tricky questions. Anything that comes into our mind can be solved with a quick search on Google. The name of the lead singer from an obscure rock band from the 1960s can be found in seconds. This is true of sets of core values too. It is so easy to use Google to find sets of core values and see if they are useful.

The exercises set out earlier in this chapter are really valuable ways of tapping into our intuition and finding out what lies deep within us and I would strongly advocate that you attempt them, both on your own and as a group process.

However, sometimes it does help to have a bit of a head start. To have the "here's one I made earlier" approach up your sleeve in case you draw a blank, or you need something to get you started.

There are plenty of examples of core value sets. Indeed, when I use Google to search for "Core Values" it identifies over six million hits. Amongst these are the core values of countless companies around the world. I suspect that a lot of these have been developed with minimal input from the staff that work in those companies. From a Google search it is also easy to bring up some

66664977

588

with. Here is one set:

Dependable

Reliable

Loyal

Committed

Open-minded

Consistent

Honest

Efficient

Innovative

Creative

Humorous

Fun-loving

Adventurous

Motivated

Positive

Optimistic

Inspiring

Passionate

Respectful

Athletic

Fit

Courageous

Educated

Respected

Loving

Nurturing

There are also sets of values that have been developed by organisations with a strong ethical interest. In some cases, these are grounded in religion. One useful example is the '16 Guidelines for a Happy Life' which has been developed by The Foundation for Developing Compassion and Wisdom. This is worth looking at in more detail and there are courses available too. The 16 core values identified in this approach are:

How we think:

Humility

Patience

Contentment

Delight

How we act:

Kindness

Honesty

Generosity

Right speech

How we relate to others:

Respect

Forgiveness

Gratitude

Loyalty

How we find meaning:

Aspiration

Principles

Service

Courage

Searching through other sets of core values can be a really helpful way to develop your own. If you work in a company or organisation that already has its own values, you need to take account of those. But for the values set to truly guide you on your path it needs to be incorporated into what you do, how you do it, and why you do it.

Stuart Eglin

Chapter 3
How many values and how to share them

Like so many things in the workplace — business plans, strategies — there is no point in developing them if we just put them in a drawer or leave them to languish on a computer hard drive. In this chapter, we will look at what happens next.

Now you have a list

So, you have worked through some of the approaches suggested in the previous chapter, and now you have a list of core values. How many are there? Do you have a refined list of three key values or do you have an extensive list of forty-three different characteristics that are at the core of everything that you do?

There is no right number, no correct list of values. It needs to be very much driven by what you are doing, where you are working and how you will use this list. However, if the list is too short it probably doesn't reflect properly the range of issues that will underpin decisions about the work you do and determining your future direction. So, only having three values is probably not helpful. At the other end of the spectrum, a list of forty-three different values is probably way too large. It will be impossible to remember, and therefore it will not really drive you forward in your work and daily living. In chapter two I described the six core values that underpin the work of the team which I lead. That list of six is relatively easy to remember. It is also straightforward to map it back to the work that we do, and the overarching themes of our work.

The list of values can be tracked back to the mission statement that summarises our work.

So, whilst there is no right answer to this, it is pretty clear that the number of values that come from the exercises needs to be manageable for the group that work with them. They need to also be recognisable, which is why I don't advocate the idea of adopting a list from elsewhere.

It may be useful to put the list on a card so that it is available to refer to if required. However, this should only be done if it is clearly useful to the people who are going to use it. Let me tell you a story about how not to develop values and work them into an organisation. I once worked in an organisation which employed approximately 100 people. It was a public sector organisation and we were told that we had to pursue Investors in People (an accreditation process which assesses the extent to which you have good people practises in place for your employees) within a very tight timescale. One member of staff was tasked with getting us ready. This entailed printing up large boards with a mission statement and key values for the organisation. No staff had seen these values before they appeared on the walls. They were posted up the day before we were due to be assessed. We passed that stage of the accreditation process because everyone was familiar with the mission and core values. However, the level of credibility of the process was zero. There was no ownership of the process or the values themselves.

Without proper engagement in the process and a measured process which takes everyone along at pace, the development of a value set will be worthless.

Reviewing your values

The values developed in chapter two are a few years old now. We developed them originally in 2011. They are still very much in use today even though the team has gone through many changes. People have come and gone, the organisation that we worked in has been abolished and the work that we do has changed significantly. Does this mean that it is important to hold onto the core values regardless? Well, to some extent that is true. The idea of working from a strong set of values and beliefs stems from the sense that they help to propel us forwards. They will determine how we set our direction, they will influence how and who we recruit to the team. In my own example, the core values helped us to survive the abolition of our host organisation and navigate our way to a new structure and hosting arrangement. But that doesn't mean that we should hold onto the values regardless and keep using them blindly. It is really important to review the value set regularly. My team has reviewed our values at least once a year. Each time we begin by going through the values and making sure that the whole team understands what we mean by each word, how we turn that value into practise in our work. Then, we take time to look at whether that still works for us. We also take time to consider whether there is anything missing from our core values that we need to take account of. To date, our values haven't changed since we first set them.

But there have been times when we did look closely at them and really challenge whether they were still appropriate. For example, a couple of years ago when we did a detailed review we spent time looking at the values of inclusivity and co-creation. To us, these meant that we share openly our work and working practises. We also aim to work with partners to develop new ideas together.

We took a long time to work through these ideas to see whether they still worked for us. We were surrounded by organisations where the ethos was grounded in competition.

Some team members felt that we were having our ideas taken and used by others with credit. It really challenged our value set. Should we continue to be so open and sharing in the way that we worked if it wasn't serving us?

After a long debate, we concluded that we could still hold to these values. It was core to the way that we work that we should co-create with others. We just needed to be clear about who we shared what with, and at what stage in development. To take a phrase which Margaret Wheatley introduced me to in a Skype call in preparation for a workshop that she ran with the team:

"Hold your ideas close until you are ready to share. Don't be naïve."

It was great advice.

This felt like a time where the challenges of the environment around us were really pushing us and making us question our values. But the more we discussed it, the clearer we were that we would continue to hold true to our values. It was a powerful learning process.

Sharing your values

I described earlier a really bad approach to sharing values where the organisation imposed a value set on its staff and stuck boards up on the wall to tell people what the values were. It's a shame that this approach was not handled more sensitively, because the sharing of values is really important.

Once you have a set of values, they should be visible and available for all to see. I would suggest putting them in a prominent place on your website, in any corporate documents you produce such as annual reports, prospectuses, operational plans etc.

Make sure that the team have easy access to the values so that they can be referred to when appropriate.

You could also consider sharing values through social media.

A couple of words of caution with this. Do make sure that the value set you are describing is congruous with what you are doing. Sharing values through social media can backfire really badly if you say that you espouse the values of honesty and transparency whilst having offshore investment arrangements that avoid paying tax!

Also, if you have conducted the various steps described to define your values and the team are now highly engaged – there is the danger that this work will tip over into evangelism. There is no problem having a highly engaged team of people who are really passionate about what they are doing and believe really strongly in the values set that they have developed. Just be careful not to evangelise the values and repel potential partners and clients. The value set should underpin what you do, not overshadow it.

Ways you can use values

You have shared your values widely so that others know what underpins your work. You have been cautious not to shout about them. And you intend to review them regularly.

That is all good, but what about practical uses for the values that you have developed? Should they be something that just sits beneath the surface and helps to steer how you do things or should it be more explicit than that? For core values to have real merit they should be something that can be brought to the team by anyone. Thus, in a team discussion about a new work area, or a decision about moving premises, or a financial decision – you know that you have got really powerful values that everyone is working with when someone other than the leader refers to them and asks whether a particular value can help in reaching a decision.

The value set can also help with planning work that the team needs to do. My team has an annual planning cycle, like most. We get together once a year to set the direction for the following year – in that process we would look to be driven the value set. We are also just beginning to set aside a day each month for 'Rehearsal Time' when the team is not available to the outside world unless we invite them in. Although we are calling this Rehearsal Time, we are not working in the theatre, we are just using the term to describe a closed space where we are not on show. Like many teams a lot of our work in delivering workshops, conferences and seminars does involve us" being on show". It is important that we also have time when we can work privately.

In this time we are working on how we work together, what we are working on, and new ideas. Afternoons are deliberately unstructured to encourage creative thinking and innovation. We also have a process of capture for each day including photos, video and blogging. This encourages us to be self-reflective during the day. Hopefully that also leads to wider reflective practises throughout the month. The value set we work with is key to these Rehearsal Days.

After working with a set of core values for a while, their use in the everyday practise of the team should become quite natural. They are referred to in passing as an indicator to aid decisions, inform the way we work together and help with the overall direction we are travelling.

Chapter 4
Consolidating as people come and go

I have already mentioned in the previous chapter that the values we work with need to be adaptable to the changing circumstances in which we work. They also need to be available and accessible to new people as they join the team.

With a flexible approach, we are able to enrich and deepen the value set that we work with so that it becomes a beacon illuminating our working practises.

Future proofing and flexing

We also need to be sure that we use the value set in a way that ensure that we are future proofing what we do. It is important not to just chase the contracts, follow where the money is. Once we have worked out what it is that we are there to do, we can be much clearer about the purpose of the work that we are doing. Then we can judge each opportunity that arises and make sure that it is congruent with our values.

We need to be a combination of flexible and strong. Like the tree that stands alone, not shielded by the other trees in the forest. The strongest tree isn't the one that is rigid, it is the tree that flexes and bends in the wind. Similarly our approach to work needs to reflect this mixture of the strength that comes from being really clear about our value base, whilst also being flexible and open to opportunity.

Introducing new team members to the values set

When new members join the team, it is vital that the core values are identified early. Ideally, they should be articulated in the recruitment material that is used. This is the first opportunity to set out clearly what the values of the team are and make clear to potential candidates what drives the work and the value base with which they will need to be congruent.

Once appointed, the leader needs to work through the values with the new member of staff as a part of the induction process. This is an opportunity for the new person to check out the meaning of the values and how they are applied by the team.

It is probably also worth ensuring that there is a team discussion that encompasses values soon after the new person starts so that they can see how the values of the team are used in practise.

Values can overshadow the team

I can almost hear you thinking to yourself, "OK, Stuart. You've set out this whole concept of values-based working and you have made it clear just how important it is. Then, you have gone into detail about the way to build up a set of core values within a team. But isn't there a danger that this becomes such an obsession that we don't get anything done in the meantime?"

It's a good point. I am not suggesting that core values should eclipse or overshadow all that we do. They sit at our core and are there to drive our actions. When we work with those values we feel positive and that everything is in flow. When we don't we can feel high levels of stress and discomfort.

But we are able to work with situations that compromise our values. It is just that we should avoid that when we can. Understanding what our core values are is a good way to ensure that we are conscious of the drivers that help us to stay congruent.

With all of this in mind, it is still critical that we do not allow the core values that drive us to become such an obsession that they blur our view of the team of people that we are working with. I have worked extensively in the field of public engagement and involvement. It's a vital area of public sector working which ensures that the services we provide are properly connected to the end user, and that there is authentic involvement in all aspects of the service delivery by the end user. This is an area where the existence of core values to underpin work can be both vital and also hugely challenging. Frequently the value set which is used by the initiative can be at odds with the value sets that the member of the public who acts as the advocate brings with them. This can take sensitive handling. It is important to maintain a clear focus on the individuals involved in this difference of perspective. Core values can be brought into alignment if we shift the focus to the issue that is being addressed and look at the core values that are at odds within that context. By that, I mean that we mustn't lose sight of the individuals involved − it becomes a case of looking at where the compromises need to happen to get the best outcome.

Values in our working practises

How do I use the core values that we have defined for the team with which I work?

As already described, we go through regular review of the values to ensure that they remain relevant and to ensure that we are reminded of them.

They are often referred to in team meetings and in 1:1 conversations. As we work through the programme of work that we are delivering, we will frequently look at the values and ensure that we are aligned in what we do.

New challenges are a particularly good space for using core values.

For example, a few months ago we moved the team into new premises a short walk from the existing office space. This was necessary to reduce our overheads. The process was straightforward. To set it in motion I set out three specific factors that would frame the search for new premises. These were:

The new accommodation should be no worse than our current accommodation in terms of quality. (We were in high quality offices before – the working environment we are located in has a high impact on morale and productivity).

We needed to be within easy walking distance of railway stations, and not create a significantly worse travel to work for any member of the team.

We needed to reduce the costs of our accommodation by at least 20%.

These criteria were a great focus for the property search. They were informed by our core values. And the decision itself was also informed by the values.

I have also used the core values to support development of new work areas, to help me to decide who to collaborate with, to clarify any future direction for the team's work. If you have effective core values, it is like having a thermometer, barometer and navigation system all combined together to help guide you as you walk through the challenges that life throws at you.

Stuart Eglin

Chapter 5
Core values in big business

In this chapter I will set out some examples of other companies where the core values are a really intrinsic part of the way they operate, and I will also show you examples where those values have created real challenges either for the company as a whole, for its founders, or for its employees.

Innocent Drinks

Innocent Drinks began in 1999 when three graduates from Cambridge University in England developed the idea for a company that would make healthy smoothie drinks from fresh ingredients. It was a great idea, that was complemented by a really effective branding, packaging and marketing approach that presented the company as a quirky supplier with an eye on the environment and health. The packaging of its drinks had bold statements about the intention of the company.

All of this looked to the customer like a big statement about the core values that underpinned the company. If asked to guess, the average customer would probably say that they were a compassionate company with their eyes on the impact of their product on the environment, that they were intent on only using fresh ingredients to ensure that the customer's health was enhanced by the product. They also established the Innocent Foundation to invest a percentage of profits into charitable work. In the early stages of the business, that seemed to be a winning formula. The company grew very fast and became a much talked-about enterprise with high credentials from an ethical perspective.

That all started to go wrong when the three founding partners sought further finance to grow the business. They agreed to sell a 10% stake in the business to Coca-Cola and almost immediately they found themselves at the heart of controversy.

According to Rob Harrison, editor of Ethical Consumer magazine:

"Innocent was never the most ethical smoothie company... this accolade went to companies using extensively Fairtrade or organic ingredients. Innocent did however have a distinct social mission which may be eroded on this new partnership with Coca-Cola." Coca-Cola have been criticised particularly for links with:

- water extraction impacts on local communities in developing countries

- suppression of trade union activity in Colombia

- sale of unhealthy drinks products to children.

What were they thinking! From a commercial perspective the decision looked like a good one – the company has continued to grow massively albeit in return for Coca-Cola's stake growing to 90%. But what had happened to the core mission and values that the business was founded upon?

In an interview with The Guardian newspaper the founders of the company, talking as they did the deal with Coca-Cola said:

"Every promise that Innocent has made, about making only natural healthy products, pioneering the use of better, socially and environmentally aware ingredients, packaging and production techniques, donating money to charity and having a point of view on the world will remain," co-founder Richard Reed yesterday. "We'll just get to do them even more. The founders will continue to lead and run the company, we will be the same people in the same offices making the same products in the same way." That hasn't been the case at all. It's such a shame to see the ideals and high values that could have taken a company forward in a powerful way being abandoned in return for significant growth.

If you look at their website today there is still a significant amount of information about their ethics and the charitable foundation which they support. It is difficult in this though to see the difference between genuine values and branding. When you look at the fuller picture, the story they tell of the history of the company feels so much like an air-brushed version of the facts.

Ben & Jerry's Ice Cream

The American ice cream company, Ben & Jerry's was founded in 1978 by Ben Cohen and Jerry Greenfield. It developed a clean living image, led by the two founders who come from the free-living idealist generation that grew up in the 1960s. Their ice cream was packaged as purely natural and kind to the environment. A similar picture to that developed by Innocent two decades later. In 1994 a book was written by Fred Lager, former CEO, about the Ben & Jerry's story. In it he claimed that he would tell how "Two Real Guys Built a Business with a Social Conscience and a Sense of Humour".

The social conscience, or in my terms a strong set of core values meant that the founders of the business frequently used the company as a platform for protest about issues they cared about. In 2010, when they appointed a new CEO who had worked previously at Unilever, he said that "values led businesses can play a critical role in driving positive change. We need to lead by example, and prove to the world that this is the best way to run a business." Unilever had acquired the company back in 2001. Up to that point Ben & Jerry's had worked with sustainable, Fair Trade certified and organic suppliers. They used environmentally friendly packaging, paid premium prices to dairy farmers from Vermont who did not give their cows growth hormones and created business opportunities for depressed areas and disadvantaged people. They gave 7.5% of their pre-tax revenues to charity. At the time of the acquisition, however, the Ben & Jerry's alternative management style lacked the fiscal and managerial discipline market analysts and investors demanded. One can only imagine some of the heated discussions that would have taken place in the boardroom as the Unilever culture moved into this small-town USA company and worked to make changes.

An online search today to see what has happened to Ben & Jerry's does, on the surface, suggest that the company has maintained a lot of its key values. Its Wikipedia page is much more positive and upbeat than that of Innocent. But is that just because Unilever and Ben & Jerry's are so much better at protecting and managing their brand? Taking a deeper look, it becomes apparent that the founders Ben Cohen and Jerry Greenfield have maintained a major role in the business. They are still leading on big causes. For example, they publicly supported the Occupy Wall Street Movement.

In an interview Jerry Greenfield said "We get a lot of support - sometimes I'm a little surprised at how supportive Unilever is. I don't know that I would say that Ben & Jerry's is a big influence on Unilever - Ben & Jerry's is like a flea on the back of this giant thing," he says.

It is hard to distinguish any effect that the acquisition may have had from the way that the whole of the business world has gone over the past dozen years.

Jerry Greenfield says he doesn't care why companies are launching such programmes.

"Some companies may feel like they need to do it because they're getting pressured by consumers, but for whatever reason they're doing it, it makes me happy. I don't care if they're doing it to look good or to make their wives happy or whatever - it's a good thing."

"It's easy to think of making money and then you give some away and you're a good company," he says.

"But the real power of a business is in how it conducts its everyday operations and integrating environmental concerns right in the day-to-day activities: how you source your ingredients, your banking relationships, your marketing, all these activities."

On the face of it, Ben & Jerry's looks like a company where the core values have survived the major shift that happened when a major multi-national company took over. The resilience of the founders of the company in maintaining those values and doggedly fighting for what they believe to be right has kept the company true to those wild aspirations they had right back at the start.

RV, the film

Have you seen the film "RV" starring Robin Williams? It's a very funny film with an underlying message. I mention the film because it looks at the issues we have been considering in the previous two examples from a very different perspective.

The character in the film played by Robin Williams (Bob Munro) is going through something of a crisis. He has a massively dysfunctional family — his wife and two teenage children have lost the ability to communicate properly as a family. As Bob Munro tells his wife, "We watch TV in four separate rooms and I.M. (Instant Message) each other when it's time to eat dinner". There is a whole plot line which looks at how renting an RV (Recreation Vehicle, or what we would call a motor home in the UK) and travelling together over a long distance brings the family together through all of the crises and disasters they encounter on the way.

The journey is necessary because Bob Munro has to go to a meeting for his company to negotiate the take-over of a small drinks company. His job is to persuade the owners, who have strong values and beliefs that it is in their interests to be taken over by the larger company.

In the climax of the movie, Bob makes an impassioned speech where he is supposed to persuade the company owners to sign the deal. Instead, he tells them that it is not in their interests to 'merge' the Alpine Soda Company with his own company. He resigns his job and walks out, leaving the meeting in disarray and heads off with his family.

It's not the greatest movie ever, the critics panned it. I like it because it made me laugh out loud. And I really liked the messages in the film. It doesn't go into immense depth about the issue of working with values, but the message is clear enough. The stark difference between the two companies was never going to be a good match. The larger company clearly wants the smaller one, because they can see a business opportunity. They are not interested in the wholesome values of the Alpine Soda Company.

The similarities to the story of Ben & Jerry's is not an accident. It's interesting to compare what happens in the film to the real-life case study that is playing out between Ben & Jerry's and Unilever, which has more than its fair share of controversies to deal with. At the time of writing this book, there are petitions circulating on the internet about Unilever's alleged pollution in India from a plant that leaked mercury into the waterways locally. Whilst acknowledging the problem, the company has been slow to compensate.

Stuart Eglin

Chapter 6
Value Based or Faith Based – are they the same thing?

In the last chapter we looked at the stories of a couple of real companies and the path they took as they grew and the need for financial backing and business acumen meant that they had to consider investment from a larger company that didn't share the same values base. It's a salutary tale that too often this ends in disaster for the founding principles of the smaller company. In the examples I gave, there is a positive outcome for Ben & Jerry's and a mixed picture for Innocent.

Let us now look at a story about a small company based in Maine, USA. I first came across this story back in the 1990s when I was studying for a PhD. I was looking for companies that used strong narrative techniques to underpin the way they worked. I had come across a few examples of this. I was also interested in companies where there was a strong value set. Luckily for me, the founder of the company Tom's of Maine had written a book about his experiences setting up a company with his wife Kate and developing it into a business with really strong core values. It's a great book, well worth a read. In "The Soul of a Business" Tom Chappell describes the path he took to develop his business with a strong set of beliefs underpinning it.

Those beliefs, set out in the book in 1993, have barely changed and are still prominently set out on the company's website today. Here they are:

Tom's of Maine statement of beliefs:

We believe that both human beings and nature have inherent worth and deserve our respect

We believe in products that are safe, effective, and made of natural ingredients.

We believe that our company and our products are unique and worthwhile, and that we can sustain these genuine qualities with an ongoing commitment to innovation and creativity.

We believe that we have a responsibility to cultivate the best relationships possible with our coworkers, customers, owners, agents, suppliers and community.

We believe that different people bring different gifts and perspectives to the team and that a strong team is founded on a variety of gifts.

We believe in providing employees with a safe and fulfilling work environment and an opportunity to grow and learn.

We believe that competence is an essential means of sustaining our values in a competitive marketplace.

We believe our company can be financially successful while behaving in a socially responsible and environmentally sensitive manner.

We believe that we have an individual and collective accountability to the Company's beliefs, mission, destiny, and performance goals.

There is also a Mission Statement:

Tom's of Maine mission:

To serve our customers by providing safe, effective, innovative natural products of high quality.

To build relationships with our customers that extend beyond product usage to include full and honest dialogue, responsiveness to feedback, and the exchange of information about products and issues.

To respect, value, and serve not only our customers but also our coworkers, owners, agents, suppliers, and community; to be concerned about and contribute to their well-being; and to operate with integrity so as to be deserving of their trust.

To provide meaningful work, fair compensation, and a safe, healthy work environment that encourages openness, creativity, self-discipline, and growth.

To contribute to and affirm a high level of commitment, skill, and effectiveness in the work community.

To recognize, encourage, and seek a diversity of gifts and perspectives in our worklife.

To acknowledge the value of each person's contribution to our goals and to foster teamwork in our tasks.

To be distinctive in products and policies which honor and sustain our natural world.

To address community concerns, in Maine and around the globe, by devoting a portion of our time, talents, and resources to the environment, human needs, the arts, and education.

To work together to contribute to the long-term value and sustainability of our company.

To be a profitable and successful company while acting in a socially and environmentally responsible manner.

To create and manage a system of accountability which holds each person in the Company's employment or governance responsible for individual behavior and personal performance consistent with the

Company's Beliefs, Mission, Destiny, Performance Goals, and Individual Work Plans.

That's an impressive set of values and beliefs. Those values were originally developed in 1989 during a company retreat. Tom describes the process of developing them in what was a very participative exercise.

The Tom's of Maine story - just like the others?

This is starting to sound like a familiar story: founders of a small company, driven by strong values that come from their desire to see a certain product. They can't find that product in the marketplace, so to solve "the itch" they decide to do it themselves. With his wife they raised funds back in 1970 to set up a company that would make laundry detergent that didn't contain phosphates. They quickly diversified making products like toothpaste and deodorants from entirely natural products, no chemicals. In the early stages of the business they sell the product through health food stores. Then, as they grow they realise that they will need to diversify and sell through supermarkets, bringing them into direct competition with big businesses like Procter and Gamble. The book describes how Tom and Kate built the business, how they forged the way with their company and took on each challenge that growth brought to the business they were in. Tom also describes many of the techniques and approaches he adopts to ensure the success of the business whilst building a strong community of employees as well as strong links with the wider community in which they are based. They establish many charitable endeavours and agree to give 10% of profits to their charity work. They also make it possible for the workforce to do charitable work within their paid time for the company.

The spiritual journey - Tom studies Divinity

There is a point in the company's evolution when Tom realises he is unhappy, that making more and more money is not satisfying. In his own words: "Why was I so unhappy? Because my everyday business life had gone stale. Work had become an unfulfilling exercise. I felt empty, disconnected from my company and my self. I called myself an entrepreneur but I hadn't created a new product in five years. The young professionals I had hired to help me grow the company were taking Tom's of Maine in directions that I was not sure I wanted it to go. I was still making the numbers, but I was beginning to think twice about the personal and professional meaning of work, money, possessions, power and prestige. I considered cashing in, selling the company, and retiring at age forty-three." He didn't do that. Instead he decided that he should do a Masters degree in Divinity part-time. It was a bold move, something that few business leaders would consider. It did what he was hoping it would. Through his studies he realised a deeper purpose to the work of leading the company. He came across the work of Martin Buber and Jonathan Edwards, which helped to give him a strong philosophical basis to the values-based approach he had been striving to achieve. This helped to drive forward the mission of Tom's of Maine with a deeper purpose and philosophical underpinning to everything that they were achieving. He references the work of the Quakers too in the phrase "do well by doing good". He describes the epiphany that he realised as being the middle way where we use our head and heart in planning business strategies. The book uses a lot of language that comes from faith traditions. Tom became actively involved in the Episcopal Church in Maine. The Middle Way is a Buddhist concept, although it is also found in other faith traditions.

To what extent is the spiritual journey of Tom Chappell driving the core values of the company? Does it have a significant impact on the workforce? Is it possible to have a strong values base that is faith-agnostic?

Colgate-Palmolive buy the business

In 2006 Colgate-Palmolive bought a controlling 84% stake in Tom's of Maine for $100 million. What changed? In the book Tom describes approaches from his major competitors and states clearly that they were all rejected because he didn't want to compromise what the company stood for.

After many years of substantial growth, he describes the massive challenges he was facing at the time of writing the book. Western capitalism is so connected to the idea of permanent growth that a company is considered to be failing at risk of being taken over if it is not sustaining continued growth. But this model is clearly at odds with the founding principles of Tom's of Maine, as well as Innocent and Ben & Jerry's.

Looking at the story of Tom's of Maine, and all the information they have on their website it does look like they managed to achieve a carefully crafted deal with their new owners that would protect the values (they haven't changed) and protect the stewardship principles of the company.

Tom and Kate are less involved now — they are on to the next venture called Ramblers Way (another eco-friendly company, this time selling wool clothing). Their website espouses the same values that drove Tom's of Maine. In selling out to Colgate-Palmolive, Tom Chappell said:

"We'll be a stand-alone subsidiary, and we have a commitment from Colgate that our formulas will not be tampered with. Colgate-Palmolive of New York plans to keep the Tom's of Maine brand name and hopes to use its significant distribution network and marketing muscle to boost sales. With annual revenue of nearly $50 million, Tom's of Maine said it can grow faster with Colgate in what Colgate estimates is a fast-growing $3 billion US market for natural oral-care and personal products." During a telephone interview, Kate Chappell, 60, offered another reason to sell:

"We're not going to be here forever, and we needed to find a good home for the company."

These quotes are from a Boston newspaper at the time of the deal. The article emphasises the clandestine nature of the deal, with Colgate's brand not appearing on any of Tom's of Maine's products.

"The challenge for Colgate is to keep Tom's uniqueness and quirkiness alive. I think the average person in a store thinks that Ben & Jerry's ice cream is still being mixed by two guys in a Vermont barn." A cynical view, and an understandable one at the time. The test of time does show that the company today still holds onto the values that were developed in the early years. So, maybe it is possible for small companies to maintain powerful sets of values whilst being owned by a much bigger conglomerate.

To quote the words which Tom Chappell chooses to close the book he wrote way back in 1993:

"Managing for profit and for common good – it works"

Chapter 7
Capitalism and the Future

For nearly a decade now we have seen unprecedented changes in the world's economies. Back in 2007 it looked like we were back on the roller-coaster of change that was causing us to drop into a recession, but this time it felt so different. There had been something a little like it back in the 1930s when economies dropped into a depression that took several years to recover from. Banks collapsed, massive levels of unemployment occurred, currencies became unstable and inflation ran out of control.

This time though, there were banks that failed, but in most cases governments around the world stepped in to protect banks, bailed them out with massive injections of cash and did all that they could to ensure that these institutions which were deemed too big to fail, didn't collapse.

Many commentators have been questioning for some time now whether we are witnessing the eventual demise of capitalism. The freedom of the markets has been a dominant economic force across the world for a century or more, and in that time we have seen some remarkable achievements from its paradigm. But the increasing globalisation of companies, the growing gap between the rich and the poor, and the extent to which we have lost the battle for the planet's future do mean that we are watching the systems that we thought would protect us are breaking down. In this fractured and increasingly unpredictable world, it is ever more important to work with strong core values.

There are conflicting views about what caused the financial crisis in 2007, but it is clear that at the heart of it was a problem with rampant greed and increasingly risky financial models that looked more like the workings of a casino than something that should be seen in a responsible financial institution.

It caught us all sleep walking, thinking that we had discovered an economic approach that meant the world's leading stock markets could continue to grow and expand, that the developing world would contribute to this and grow too. It all seemed too good to be true.

The biggest religion in the world was the God of Growth; wedded to the idea that we could continue with indefinite growth we designed all our financial and economic systems with that in mind. We were also duped by the presence of social responsibility programmes. Companies had all developed their own programmes, sometimes in response to government pressure, often as a part of their overall branding process. It didn't work in the way that I have described it in companies that work from a strong ethical basis. In most companies, it was a case of paying lip service to the idea of being ethical and responsible corporate citizens. Once the crash came it was only the truly values-based companies that saw the importance of their social responsibility work. Many companies cut back in these areas, reducing the scope for employees to become involved in the company's wider programmes.

Since the global crash of economies, we now have governments with massive debts created by bailing out the banking system. Or put another way, the losses in the financial sector were written off by states giving billions in liquidity and growing the debts in the public sector. Governments are broke, business taxes aren't being paid as multi-nationals chase around the globe hiding profits to avoid having to pay any tax on their turnover. Alongside the God of Growth sits another deity, the God of Austerity. These two Gods are effectively their own Yin and Yang. One works with the other, spiralling our economies into increasing levels of dysfunction. It all looks so bleak. But just as these systems are failing and we are feeling increasingly alienated by the world around us, it is important to remember that the complexity of the world is such that we cannot control it. Just as one force works against us, there will be another that counter-balances it.

What do I mean by this? Well, the internet brought opportunities for businesses to trade globally, to be nimble and out of reach of nation's chasing taxes. But that same infrastructure brought the opportunity to connect communities of people globally. We are seeing powerful movements forming through online petitions. These organisations, often very loosely structured, feel like a new era of social movements. Groups like Change.org, SumofUs and 38 Degrees are challenging the status quo. They are engaging those who feel disengaged with traditional politics. They are creating the medium through which to deliver global accountability and democracy.

These groups are a way of connecting disparate people around a cause. They offer opportunities for anyone to put up an online petition and seek support from others. Values based campaigning is a massive force that can have a serious impact on governments and can change policies.

Capitalism is a very resilient system. It has lasted a relatively long time. Although let us not forget that some of the political systems that preceded it lasted vastly longer than capitalism has.

Is capitalism broken beyond repair? Will it unravel in the years to come? I doubt we have seen the end of capitalism. But as we see the shift from the industrial age, to the information age, and now to the social age — there will be massive and seismic change. We are already seeing this. But consider that already massive companies like Google,

Facebook and Apple are predicting that the online community will grow enormously as more people in developing nations come online. With that change in the level of connectedness it is encouraging to see that online communities are looking at ways to embed strong social values. For every instance of trolling, there are many examples of social media being used for good. Online petitions, charity giving, raising awareness of injustices are all examples of the way that our basic humanity can achieve so much.

Working with a strong value base, and being clear how we can improve things around us, and make a real contribution to the world should fill us with hope.

These are crazy times, times when it is impossible to predict with any certainty what the future will look like — but there is hope thanks to the efforts of those who work with a strong values base.

Chapter 8
The Existential Question

"The two most important days in your life are the day you were born, and the day you find out why." Mark Twain

There is one big question, bigger than all the others. One question that we spend a lifetime trying to figure out. Whether we are an atheist, an agnostic or follow a faith, this question still preoccupies us. What are we here for? What is our life's purpose?

In this chapter I will describe my own personal quest to pursue this big question and try to figure out the answer. In my teenage years I began to wonder about this. Sometimes the question was prompted by that question that we are asked so often when we are at school. What do you want to be when you grow up? I joke about this now – saying, I am still not sure I know what I want to do when I grow up!

I was brought up a Christian in a family that attended church regularly. My journey through faith has taken me through a lot of searching. I now consider myself a Buddhist. Whilst following that path I have read widely and my searching has generated more questions than it has answered.

In my late teens and early 20s I found that writing was a great way to make sense of things. It was as though the answers came through as I wrote. Many writers talk of channelling what they write from some source, which they don't quite understand. Over the years I have found writing in journals and writing poetry has really helped me to understand 'what I am here for'. Also, in the many jobs I have done I have always been bemused by the way that whatever it is that drives me, comes through regardless of the job. Somehow a force within me converts any job with flexibility in it to something that fits what I am here to do.

Through my 30s and 40s I would be attracted to certain jobs, and would then shape and mould them so that I was able to work with those core values that were deep within me.

As I grew older I realised that there were people around me who had identified their life's purpose. There seemed to be a strong congruence about the way they worked. It was impressive. I wished that I had that clarity. My relatively unfocused approach to life was, I thought, a significant disadvantage. Nonetheless I did what I could to act "as if" I had that congruence. I did a lot of searching for ideas that worked for me. I was bold and chased the maddest ideas if they had appeal. It is so true, that if we keep on acting as if, eventually it has sunk so deep within us, that we have an authenticity too. Something that began as an act, becomes genuinely baked into our character. It was like the story of the Ugly Duckling. I realised one day that I was working to my life's purpose. It had crept up on me without me noticing. I could tell this, because when I spoke about the work I was doing and really got in touch with the values that drove the work, I would speak with a passion which surprised me as much as the listener. My purpose was speaking from my core, and using me as a vessel to communicate. And that is where this book began with the identifying of 6 core values to drive the work that I am now doing.

Stuart Eglin

Chapter 9
Endgame

I had a "strategic latté" in Lancaster a few months ago with a new contact. This is a key part of how I work. I am always looking for new ideas and interesting conversations. Having a coffee in an informal setting is a great way to do that. We were meeting for a chat and to learn about the approach that each of us was taking. Stephen was running a small social enterprise providing services to support independent living. We ended up talking about the importance of values. We realised as the conversation developed that values are key to underpinning the work that we do and driving forward major decisions that we make about the work we will become involved in. We also realised that the structure of organisation is secondary to the set of values that we work from. If we have a robust set of values, the governance that we work with, whether public, private or not for profit becomes much less important. Of course, there are other considerations to take into account when deciding which organisational structure is the best fit. But it is important to realise that structure does not determine values. Values drive the structure and ensure that we are working from a sound ethical base.

Values help us to look at what we should say no to as well as what we should say yes to. They also help us to see who fits well with our work - employees, associates and partners. Above all else, being clear about the values of the organisation we are working in helps us to be clear that we have good alignment with our workplace. If this is not the case, it's probably time to start looking for another job!

The journey in this book has been from one example of setting values in a team, through practical approaches that you can try, and on to some examples of working with values in bigger companies. Then we went on to look at the bigger global context. Finally we shifted to look at the drive within us that brings us to the big questions that we all face in life.

I hope that I have convinced you through all of this that there is real value to be gained in working from a strong values base. We need to believe in what we do. We need to have clear purpose if we are to go out of this world with the vivid sense that we left it at least a little the better for us having been around.

Stuart Eglin

Chapter 10
Acknowledgements

My thanks are due to June Eglin-Lowe for believing in me even when I doubted that I could produce a book on this topic. Without June's patient support for this quest, it would never have made it to the printed form. Thank you for your support and encouragement, and thanks for being the first person to read these words. I would also like to thank some of the people who I have had the great fortune to work with in recent years, whose ideas have helped to shape mine. In particular I would like to thank Michael West, Julian Stodd, Etienne Wenger and Margaret Wheatley. Also, Dave Pollard's blog "How to save the world" was a source of inspiration 10 years ago when I first started to read blogs regularly.

The values described in the second chapter were identified through an extended piece of work with Nick Fayers and Sue Roberts, when they were working on an Impact Evaluation for the work of the team that I lead. They really helped to articulate the core values that we work to, through a series of in depth conversations which were great fun and very insightful.

The team I work with have been incredibly tolerant of me as I experiment and test things out with their involvement. Thanks to Gillian, Bill, Lynne, Jo-Anne, Leanne, Mel, Carolyn and Safeena. The work that we are doing on Michael West's Team Journey, has been facilitated by Taravandana Lupson who has kept us on track. I also really appreciate the support and boost that I have had from Su Fowler-Johnson, Kevin Wyke and Claire Harris.

Finally I would like to thank Val Michej, my coach, for her calm persistence in helping me to fight the inner critic and imposter syndrome so that I made it to the finish line and produced the book that is in your hand.

Chapter 11
Suggested Reading

Here are some books that are useful to read. Some of these authors are referred to in the text. Others have written books that I have found particularly useful.

Margaret Wheatley — Walk Out Walk On

We did a day workshop with Meg Wheatley on the importance of community. She explained how critical it is to have strong community to support us when we push the boundaries. Connecting with others is so important. We are islands of sanity in a sea of insanity.

Julian Stodd — The Social Leadership Handbook

Julian also did a day workshop with us explaining his theories about social learning. In a highly practical workshop he talked us through the importance of social connectedness in claiming the space in which we work.

Michael West – Effective Team Work

I have known Michael for 10 years now. His work on the value of teams, and his research into what makes an effective team is impressive. He has worked extensively in healthcare in England to improve team working. This is an excellent book which summarises his work. At the time of writing this, the team and I are working through a team development process which he has developed. It is a powerful programme delivered by Aston Organisation Development.

Tom Chappell – The Soul at Work

This book is the basis for chapter seven. It's a great read, full of ideas about how to build an ethical company that is truly empowering.

Robert Sardello – Facing the World with Soul

Robert Sardello is one of a group of Psychologists under the leadership of James Hillman who became known as the Archetypal Psychologists. Their work has been a massive influence on my approach. They base their work Carl Jung's archetypal theories.

Michael Gelb – How to Think Like Leonardo da Vinci

I love this book. It is a really practical book full of ideas for enhancing creativity and developing our minds. Full of practical exercises to do. One of them – the 100 questions exercise (look it up online) – is so powerful that I do it every three months and then work with the findings to focus my goals. Try it and see how it works for you.

Stuart Eglin

Chapter 12
About the Author

Stuart Eglin is:

A Husband

A Father

A Writer

A Poet

An Entrepreneur

A Leadership Coach

A Freelance Consultant

An Evaluation Expert

A Creativity Consultant

A Music Fanatic

A Music Maker

A Buddhist

A Socialist

A Free Thinker

and a host of other things too. He splits his time between working in the English National

Health Service, coaching and writing. He has written 20 books of poetry over the last three decades. He has had two of these books published as chapbooks and has had over 70 poems published by magazines in the UK and USA. He has also written a novel and two books on coaching and organisational change.

He works part-time in the NHS in England where he leads work on strategic development of health research for the North West region. He is an Honorary Visiting Professor at the University of Liverpool in the Institute of Psychology, Health and Society. He has a PhD in organisational change from Manchester Business School in which he studied the psychological aspects of change within organisations in the NHS, focusing particularly on applications of Jungian and Archetypal Psychology. He has previously held honorary appointments with the University of Manchester, Lancaster University and Liverpool John Moores University.

If you would like to contact Stuart Eglin you can email him on stuart.eglin@gmail.com and you can also follow him on his blog at www.stuarteglin.com.

Stuart Eglin

20512164R00076

Printed in Great Britain
by Amazon